ANIMALS
That Make a Difference!

Butterflies

Ashley Lee

Explore other books at:
WWW.ENGAGEBOOKS.COM

VANCOUVER, B.C.

ℓ WWW.ENGAGEBOOKS.COM

Butterflies: Level 2
Animals That Make a Difference!
Lee, Ashley 1995 –
Text © 2020 Engage Books
Design © 2020 Engage Books

Edited by: A.R. Roumanis,
Jared Siemens, and Lauren Dick
Design by: A.R. Roumanis

Text set in Arial Regular.
Chapter headings set in Arial Black.

FIRST EDITION / FIRST PRINTING

LIBRARY AND ARCHIVES CANADA CATALOGUING IN PUBLICATION

Title: Butterflies: Animals That Make a Difference Level 2 reader / Ashley Lee
Names: Lee, Ashley, 1995- author.

Identifiers: Canadiana (print) 20200308947 | Canadiana (ebook) 20200308955
ISBN 978-1-77437-626-3 (hardcover)
ISBN 978-1-77437-627-0 (softcover)
ISBN 978-1-77437-628-7 (pdf)
ISBN 978-1-77437-629-4 (epub)
ISBN 978-1-77437-630-0 (kindle)

Subjects:
LCSH: Butterflies—Juvenile literature
LCSH: Human-animal relationships—Juvenile literature

Classification: LCC QL544.2 .L44 2020 | DDC J595.78/9—DC23

Contents

What Are Butterflies?

Butterflies are flying **insects**. Their colorful wings make them easy to spot.

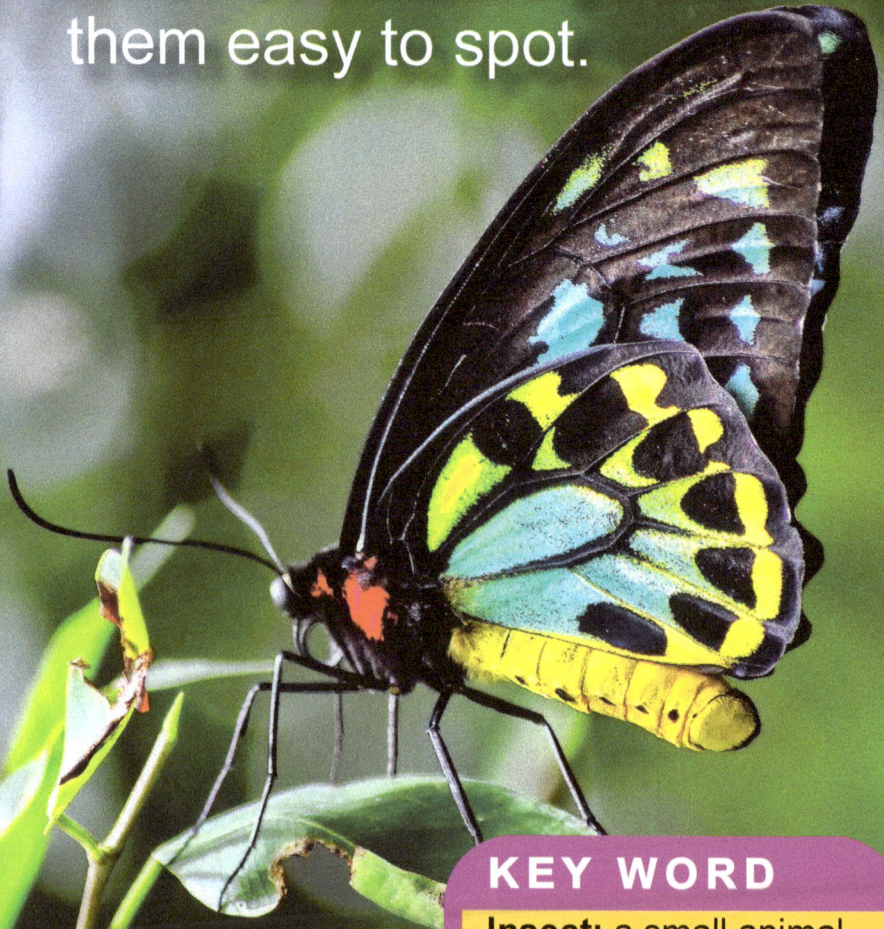

4

KEY WORD

Insect: a small animal with six legs. Its body is covered in a hard shell.

A group of butterflies is called a kaleidoscope. They are very helpful to people, other animals, and Earth.

A Closer Look

The smallest butterflies are only about 1 inch (2.5 centimeters) long with their wings stretched out. The largest butterflies can be up to 11 inches (28 cm) long.

Butterfly wings are covered in dustlike scales. These scales help keep butterflies warm.

Butterflies have two feelers on their heads called antennae. They help butterflies fly in the right direction.

Butterflies have long tongues. They are tube-shaped and act like a straw.

Where Do Butterflies Live?

Butterflies live in many different **habitats**. They can be found in tropical rainforests, deserts, and Arctic tundra. They live all over the world.

Melissa blue butterflies live in North America. Macedonian grayling butterflies only live in one village in North Macedonia. Blue morphos butterflies are mainly found in the Amazon rainforest.

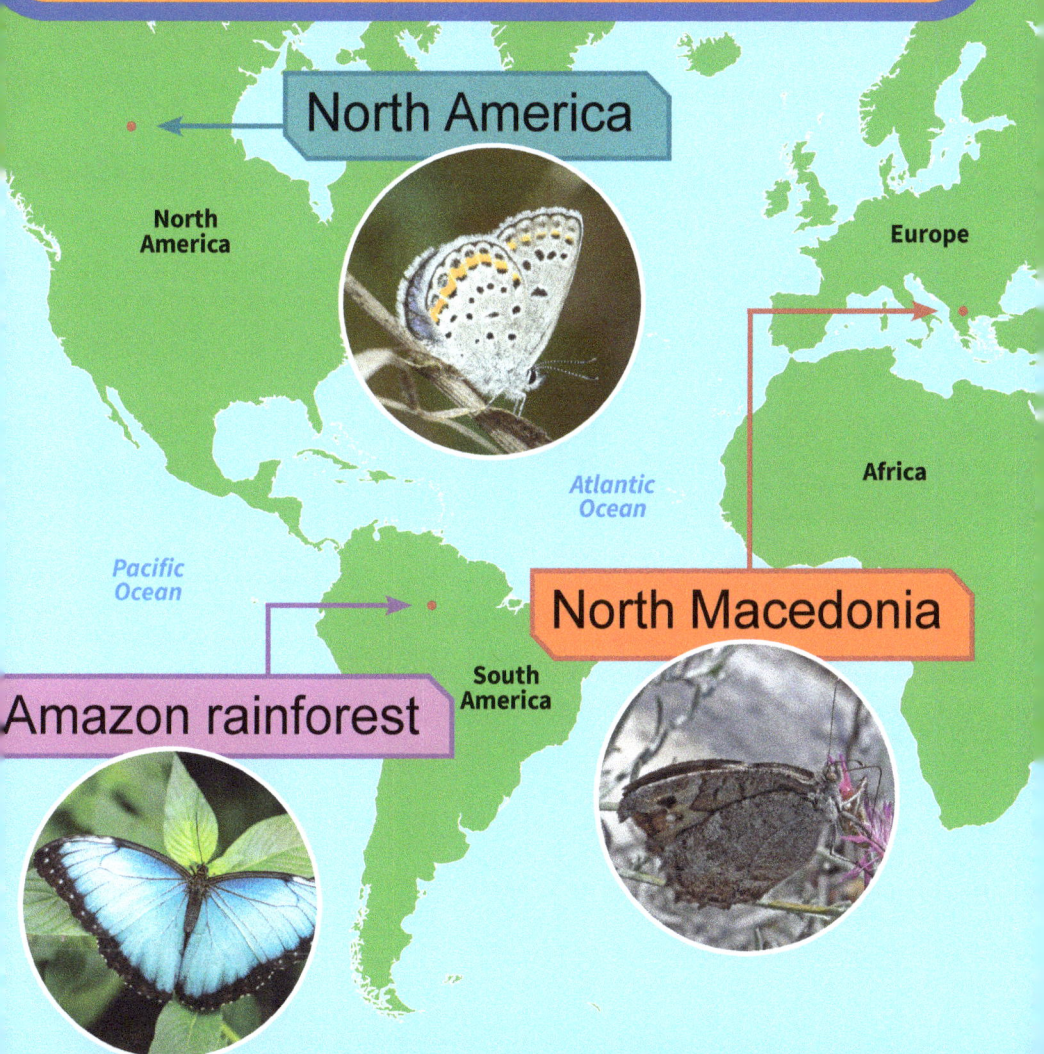

North America

North America

Europe

Atlantic Ocean

Africa

Pacific Ocean

North Macedonia

South America

Amazon rainforest

Southern Ocean

0   2,000 miles

0   4,000 kilometers

N

Legend
Land
Ocean

9

Antarctica

What Do Butterflies Eat?

Young butterflies eat leaves. Adult butterflies drink a sweet liquid from flowers called nectar. Some kinds of butterflies eat tree sap or other insects.

Some male butterflies drink from mud puddles in groups. These groups are called puddle clubs.

How Do Butterflies Talk to Each Other?

Butterflies release special chemicals called pheromones. These attract other butterflies.

Some butterflies can make noise. Male cracker butterflies make a cracking noise as they fly.

Butterfly Life Cycle

Butterflies lay their eggs on leaves. They use a sticky liquid that acts like glue. This keeps them in place.

Baby butterflies are called caterpillars. They do not have wings. Caterpillars begin eating as soon as they hatch.

Fully grown caterpillars make a hard shell called a chrysalis. The chrysalis covers the caterpillar. A caterpillar may stay in its chrysalis from a few weeks to a few months.

Caterpillars leave their chrysalides as adult butterflies. They cannot fly for at least 30 minutes.

15

Curious Facts About Butterflies

The fastest butterflies can fly 37 miles (60 km) per hour. This is faster than most dogs can run.

Some butterflies never poop. Everything they eat is used for energy.

Butterflies taste with their feet.

Butterflies can see colors humans cannot. These colors are called ultraviolet rays.

Butterflies in cold areas may stay in their hard shells for years.

A full-grown caterpillar can be 100 times larger than when it first hatched.

Kinds of Butterflies

There are more than 17,500 kinds of butterflies. They all have different markings on their wings. These markings can be any color of the rainbow.

The Monarch butterfly is known for flying south every winter. It is one of the most studied butterflies in the world.

Black swallowtail butterflies look like bird droppings when they hatch. This helps keep them safe from other animals who might eat them.

Cabbage white butterflies are some of the first butterflies to be seen in spring.

How Butterflies Help Earth

Butterflies carry **pollen** from one plant to another. Pollen helps plants make seeds. There would be less plants on Earth without butterflies.

KEY WORD

Pollen: a colorful powder that plants make.

20

Butterflies help keep farmers' crops safe. They eat the bugs that eat plants. This means that farmers do not need to use chemicals that hurt Earth to keep their crops safe.

How Butterflies Help Other Animals

Butterflies are an important food source for other animals. Birds, spiders, and frogs all eat butterflies.

Butterflies help animals when they **pollinate** plants. Many animals only eat plants. These animals would not have as much food to eat without butterflies.

How Butterflies Help Humans

Butterflies help pollinate crops that humans eat. They help fruit and vegetables grow year after year.

Some countries have started butterfly farming. They raise butterflies from eggs and sell them. Butterfly farming has created many new jobs.

Butterflies in Danger

Many butterflies are endangered. This means there are very few of them left.

The Saint Francis' satyr butterfly has been endangered since 1995. Butterfly collectors used to catch every one they found. This led to very few being left.

Some butterflies are extinct. This means there are no more of them left.

Zestos skipper butterflies went extinct in 2013. Their habitat in Florida was destroyed by growing cities.

How To Help Butterflies

People can help butterflies by planting their favorite flowers. This will give them food and a safe place to lay their eggs. Butterflies enjoy lupines, pansies, and lilacs.

Many people leave piles of leaves or fallen trees in their yard during the winter. This gives butterflies a safe place to hide until the weather gets warm.

29

Quiz

Test your knowledge of butterflies by answering the following questions. The questions are based on what you have read in this book. The answers are listed on the bottom of the next page.

1 What do butterflies eat?

2 What are baby butterflies called?

3 How do butterflies taste?

4 How do butterflies help fruits and vegetables grow?

5 What does it mean if an animal is extinct?

6 Where do butterflies hide during winter?

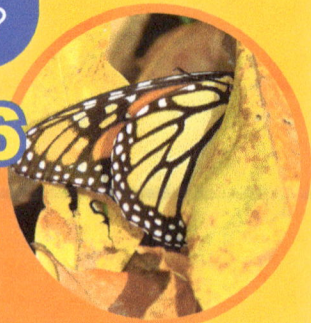

Explore other books in the Animals That Make a Difference series.

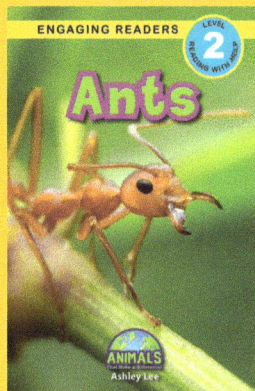

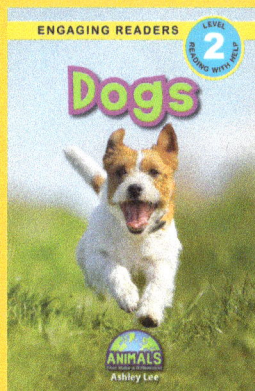

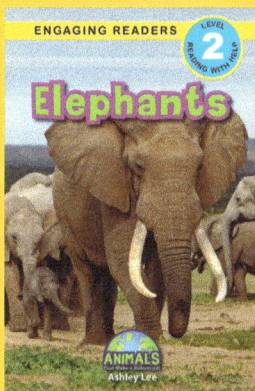

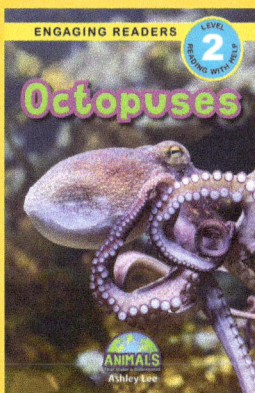

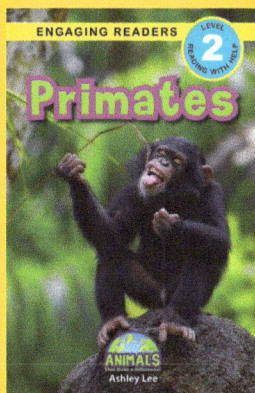

Visit www.engagebooks.com to explore more Engaging Readers.

Answers: 1. Leaves, nectar, insects, or tree sap 2. Caterpillars 3. With their feet 4. They pollinate them 5. There are no more of them left 6. In piles of leaves and under fallen trees

www.ingramcontent.com/pod-product-compliance
Lightning Source LLC
Chambersburg PA
CBHW052035030426
42337CB00027B/5011